Novels for Students, Volume 21

Project Editors: Ira Mark Milne and Timothy Sisler **Editorial**: Anne Marie Hacht

Rights Acquisition and Management: Margaret Abendroth, Margaret Chamberlain-Gaston, Edna Hedblad **Manufacturing**: Drew Kalasky

Imaging: Leitha Etheridge-Sims, Lezlie Light, Mike Logusz **Product Design**: Pamela A. E. Galbreath

Product Manager: Meggin Condino

© 2005 Gale, a part of the Cengage Learning Inc.

Cengage and Burst Logo are trademarks and Gale is a registered trademark used herein under license.

For more information, contact
Gale, an imprint of Cengage Learning
27500 Drake Rd.
Farmington Hills, MI 48331-3535

Or you can visit our Internet site at

http://www.gale.com **ALL RIGHTS RESERVED**

No part of this work covered by the copyright hereon may be reproduced or used in any form or by any means—graphic, electronic, or mechanical, including photocopying, recording, taping, Web distribution, or information storage retrieval systems—without the written permission of the publisher.

For permission to use material from this product, submit your request via Web at http://www.gale-edit.com/permissions, or you may download our Permissions Request form and submit your request by fax or mail to: *Permissions Department*
Gale, an imprint of Cengage Learning
27500 Drake Rd.
Farmington Hills, MI 48331-3535

Permissions Hotline:
248-699-8006 or 800-877-4253, ext. 8006
Fax: 248-699-8074 or 800-762-4058

Since this page cannot legibly accommodate all copyright notices, the acknowledgments constitute an extension of the copyright notice.

While every effort has been made to ensure the reliability of the information presented in this publication, Gale, an imprint of Cengage Learning does not guarantee the accuracy of the data contained herein. Gale, an imprint of Cengage Learning accepts no payment for listing; and inclusion in the publication of any organization, agency, institution, publication, service, or individual does not imply endorsement of the editors or publisher. Errors brought to the attention of the publisher and verified to the satisfaction of the publisher will be corrected in future editions.

ISBN 0-7876-6944-X
ISSN 1094-3552

Printed in the United States of America
10 9 8 7 6 5 4 3 2 1

Parable of the Sower

Octavia Butler
1993

Introduction

Parable of the Sower (New York, 1993) by Octavia Butler is set in California and covers a period of three years, from 2024 to 2027. It is a grim near-future novel that exaggerates trends in American life that were apparent in the late 1980s and early 1990s, such as fear of crime, the rise of gated communities, illiteracy, designer drugs and drug addiction, and a growing gap between rich and poor. Climate changes brought about by global warming are also central to the novel.

The protagonist is Lauren Olamina, an African American girl who is fifteen years old when the novel begins. She lives in Robledo, about twenty miles from Los Angeles, which has become a walled enclave only partially protected from the rampant lawlessness and desperate poverty that exists beyond the walls of the neighborhood. When the enclave is completely destroyed by bands of arsonists and thieves, Lauren is one of the few survivors. She heads north, on foot, with a couple of companions in a perilous search for a better life.

Butler's disturbing dystopia, written in the form of Lauren's diary entries, is at once an adventure story, a coming-of-age story, and a thought-provoking exploration of some negative trends in American society that have become more pronounced in the decade that has elapsed since the novel was written.

Author Biography

Octavia Estelle Butler was born in Pasadena, California, on June 22, 1947, the daughter of Laurice and Octavia Margaret (Guy) Butler. Her father died when she was a baby, and her mother supported the family by working as a maid. Butler loved reading science fiction stories as a child, and she soon started writing them herself. At the age of thirteen she was submitting her own stories to magazines.

Butler attended Pasadena City College, and while a student there she was awarded fifth prize in the *Writer's Digest* Short Story Contest. She received an Associate of Arts degree in 1968 and went on to attend California State University, Los Angeles, in 1969, and the University of California, Los Angeles.

In 1969, Butler entered the Open Door Program of the Screen Writers' Guild, where one of her tutors was Harlan Ellison. At Ellison's suggestion she enrolled in the Clarion Science Fiction Writers' Workshop, held in Pennsylvania. As a result of taking the workshop, she sold two short stories. Deciding she wanted to be a writer, she supported herself with low-paying jobs such as dishwashing and cleaning, while continuing to write, often getting up at three o'clock in the morning to do so. When she was laid off from a telephone sales job in 1974, she decided to use the time to write her first novel, the science fiction tale *Patternmaster*, which she completed in less than a year and sold to Doubleday. *Patternmaster* was published in 1976 and was quickly followed by three more novels in the *Patternmaster* series: *Mind of My Mind* (1977), *Survivor* (1978), and *Wild Seed* (1980). In between, Butler published *Kindred* (1979), a mainstream novel focusing on African American history.

In 1984, St. Martin's published *Clay's Ark*, a fifth volume in the *Patternmaster* series. In that year she also won the Hugo Award, for her short story "Speech Sounds," and in 1985 she won the three most prestigious science fiction awards for her novelette *Bloodchild* (1985): the Hugo Award, the Nebula Award, and the Locus Award. After this, Butler turned her attention to the science fiction trilogy, *Xenogenesis*, which was published by Warner Books. The three novels were *Dawn: Xenogenesis* (1987), *Adulthood Rites* (1988), and *Imago* (1989).

Butler then hit a barren spell. She knew she wanted to write about a woman who wanted to start a new religion, but she could not produce a manuscript that satisfied her. Eventually the ideas flowed smoothly, and the result was *Parable of the Sower* (1993).

Butler received a MacArthur fellowship in 1995. In 1998, her novel *Parable of the Talents*, which she described as a continuation of *Parable of the Sower*, was published by Seven Stories Press and republished by Warner in 2000. The novel won the Nebula Award for best novel, 1999. Also in 2000, the three novels in the *Xenogenesis* were collected under the title of *Lilith's Brood* and published by Warner Books.

Plot Summary

Chapters 1–3

Parable of the Sower begins in July 2024, in Robledo, in southern California. It is Lauren Olamina's fifteenth birthday. California has changed drastically over the past three decades. Water is scarce and expensive, there are few jobs, and climate changes have produced massive rains followed by years of drought. Lauren lives in a neighborhood that is walled off for protection from the homeless people, drug addicts, vandals, arsonists, and thieves who roam the unwalled residential areas. Lauren's father is a Baptist minister, and Lauren goes to church to be baptized, even though she no longer believes in the Christian God. The church is outside the wall, and the family goes armed. Many of the houses are burnt out and have been looted, and homeless families wander the streets. Lauren feels their pain because she suffers from "hyperempathy syndrome," also called "sharing."

Several weeks later, a neighbor named Mrs. Sims shoots herself. She was in despair after her family died in a house fire started deliberately. Meanwhile, Lauren tries to form a new concept of God. She decides that God is change, because the reality of life is that everything changes.

Chapters 4–9

In February 2025, Lauren goes to the hills with a neighborhood group for target practice, where they encounter a pack of feral dogs. They shoot one dog, and as it dies, the hyperempathic Lauren feels its pain. Guns are essential because the family cannot rely on the police to protect them. In Lauren's neighborhood, every household has at least two guns.

In March, after three-year-old Amy Dunn wanders off and is shot dead, Lauren talks with her friend Joanne Garfield about how they need to make plans to survive before their neighborhood is overrun by thieves and killers. She wants to learn how to live off the land, and she plans to create emergency packs of supplies should they have to leave in a hurry. She tries to enlist Joanne's help, but Joanne tells her parents, exaggerating what Lauren said. Lauren's father tells her to stop panicking people, but he does allow her to start teaching the neighborhood kids about her ideas.

When thieves rob the gardens, the community sets up an armed neighborhood watch. But the thieves keep coming, and Lauren is desperate to think of a way out. She develops her God-is-Change belief system further, calling it Earthseed.

Keith, Lauren' thirteen-year-old brother, slips out of the neighborhood, stealing Cory's key. He returns, beaten up. Two weeks later he disappears again for nearly two weeks. When he returns, he is wearing new clothes, but he will not say where he has been. His father beats him severely. Two months later, Keith leaves again, this time returning with money, which he gives to Cory. Then he leaves again.

Chapters 10–13

In June 2026, Keith returns after an eight-month absence. He has been squatting in an abandoned building with friends but will not say how he acquires his money. Later, he admits to robbing and shooting. In August, he is tortured and killed, probably by drug dealers.

There are more robberies, and by October the community is starting to come apart. The Garfields move to Olivar, a coastal suburb of Los Angeles, which has been bought by a company called KSF. Lauren fears that the company will cheat and abuse people. She decides that next year she will go north, maybe as far as Canada.

In November, Lauren's father disappears and is assumed dead. Lauren speaks at a church service for him, and she begins to emerge as a leader in the community. She takes over her mother's teaching responsibilities.

The day before Christmas Eve, the Olamina house is robbed. Another house, where the Payne and Parrish families live, burns down, leaving only one survivor.

Chapters 14–19

In July 2027, the entire neighborhood is overrun by violent intruders. Fires blaze everywhere. Lauren is one of the few to escape. When she returns, the place is littered with corpses, and scavengers are at work. Lauren gathers supplies, and as she leaves she meets Harry Balter and Zahra Moss. Learning that her entire family is dead, Lauren decides to head north, and Harry and Zahra go with her. Lauren cuts her hair so she can be taken for a man. They buy supplies and begin walking on the freeway, heading for the 101 that would take them up the coast toward Oregon. Hundreds of other people are walking the highways. Lauren has a gun and Harry a knife to protect themselves against predators. Lauren insists that they trust no one. At night, they take turns keeping watch. On their first night, they are attacked by two men. Lauren and Harry kill them both.

They replenish their water supplies from a commercial water station. It is a dangerous place, and Lauren and Harry help to scare off two men who attempt to rob a woman and her husband. They reach the ocean, and Lauren improves their survival skills by devising a method to make seawater drinkable. The couple they helped, Travis and Natividad, and their six-month-old baby, Dominic, join up with them, although the newcomers are suspicious at first. As the days go by, Lauren talks to her group about Earthseed. Travis and Zahra are interested, and Lauren regards Travis as her first convert.

There is an earthquake, and fire breaks out in a

community as they pass. Scavengers flock to it and there is gunfire. Lauren meets another traveler, Taylor Franklin Bankole, and he stands guard as Lauren and her friends pull two young women, Allison and her sister, Jill Gilchrist, from the rubble of a house. A man attacks Lauren, and she kills him with her knife. Allison, Jill, and Bankole travel on with Lauren's group. They reach Salinas, where they replenish their supplies, using money they have taken from corpses.

Chapters 20–25

They avoid the Bay area because the earthquake has created chaos there. Camping just east of San Juan Bautista, they emerge unscathed after a nearby gunfight at night. Bankole brings in a three-year-old child, Justin Rohr, whose mother has just been killed. Allie soon takes charge of him.

They reach the San Luis Reservoir. A friendship springs up between Lauren and Bankole, and she explains her Earthseed philosophy to him. They become lovers, and he is shocked when he finds out she is only eighteen.

By September, they reach Sacramento. They pass some horrible sights, including a dog with a child's arm in its mouth and a group of kids who are roasting a severed human leg. Bankole tells Lauren that he owns three hundred acres of land in the coastal hills of Humboldt County, where his sister lives with her husband and three children. He wants her to leave the group and go with him. Lauren thinks it might be a good place to begin the first Earthseed Community.

The group is surprised to discover that a ragged woman, Emery Tanaka Solis, and her nine-year-old daughter, Tori, have crept into their camp at night. After some discussion, the group decides to take them along with them. The next day, they are joined by Grayson Mora and his eight-year-old daughter, Doe. Grayson does not trust the group but stays for the sake of his daughter. It later turns out that Grayson, like Lauren, is a "sharer," as are Emery and Tori.

Several days later, a man tries to grab Tori and attacks Emery. Lauren shoots him, and the rest of the group fight off the remainder of the gang, but Jill is shot dead. They continue on their way, narrowly escaping a raging fire before they arrive at Clear Lake. Eventually they reach Bankole's land, but the house has been destroyed and all his family killed. They decide to stay and build Acorn, their Earthseed community.

Characters

Harry Balter

Harry Balter is a young white man from the same neighborhood as Lauren. His girlfriend is his first cousin, Joanne Garfield, but they split up when the Garfield family moves to Olivar. Harry survives the violent attack on the neighborhood and is one of the original members of Lauren's group. His new girlfriend is Zahra Moss. Harry is more trusting than Lauren, and on the road he has to learn to become more ruthless.

Taylor Franklin Bankole

Taylor Franklin Bankole is a fifty-seven-year-old black doctor who joins Lauren's group halfway through their journey. Since he is much older than the others, he is able to give them steady advice and support. Bankole is from San Diego, and he left his community after it was destroyed by arson. Five years earlier, his wife died after being beaten by thieves. Bankole and Lauren are attracted to each other and soon become lovers. He tells Lauren that he is on his way to three hundred acres of land that he owns in the coastal hills of Humboldt County, California. He hopes to meet up with his sister and her family who live there. Lauren and the group make this their destination, but when they arrive, they find that the house has been destroyed and the family killed.

Dominic Douglas

Dominic Douglas is the six-month-old son of Natividad and Travis.

Gloria Natividad Douglas

Gloria Natividad Douglas, known as Natividad, is a Hispanic woman, the wife of Travis Douglas and the mother of Dominic. This family joins Lauren's group quite early in the trek. With her husband, Natividad used to work as a maid for a rich couple, but she ran away when the man tried to seduce her.

Travis Charles Douglas

Travis Charles Douglas is a black man, the husband of Natividad. He used to work as a handyman and gardener for a rich couple. Travis is suspicious of Lauren's group at first but soon warms to them. He becomes interested in Lauren's idea of Earthseed.

Amy Dunn

Amy Dunn is a three-year-old girl in Lauren's neighborhood. She sets fire to the family garage. Later, she is accidentally shot dead.

Tracy Dunn

Tracy Dunn is Amy Dunn's sixteen-year-old mother. She was only twelve when her uncle made her pregnant with Amy. After Amy's death, Tracy disappears and is never found.

Jay Garfield

Jay Garfield is the head of the Garfield family, who are friends with the Olaminas. Jay, who is white, leads the search for Lauren's father after he disappears. Later he takes his family to the company town of Olivar.

Joanne Garfield

Joanne Garfield is the daughter of Jay Garfield, the girlfriend of Harry Balter, and Lauren's friend. Her friendship with Lauren cools when she divulges to her parents details of Lauren's plan for survival. After that, Lauren does not trust her anymore. Eventually, Joanne moves to Olivar with her parents.

Allison Gilchrist

Allison Gilchrist, known as Allie, is Jillian's twenty-five-year-old sister. After her father killed her baby because it would not stop crying, the two sisters burned the house down while the drunken father slept. Fleeing a life of prostitution and poverty, they took to the road. When Lauren's group pulls Allie and Jill out of the rubble of a house hit by an earthquake, they join the group. Allie takes charge of Justin Rohr.

Jillian Gilchrist

Jillian Gilchrist is Allison's twenty-four-year-old sister. She shares Allie's history of poverty and abuse. Neither she nor her sister can write, although they can read a little. Jill is shot dead when the group is attacked by a gang.

Bianca Montoya

Bianca Montoya is a pregnant seventeen-year-old Latino girl in Lauren's neighborhood. She plans to marry her boyfriend, Jorge Iturbe, and continue to live in the neighborhood.

Doe Mora

Doe Mora is the eight-year-old daughter of Grayson Mora.

Grayson Mora

Grayson Mora is the Latino father of Doe Mora. He joins Lauren's group toward the end of their trek. He is quiet, aloof from the group, but protective of his daughter. Like Lauren, he has hyperempathy syndrome.

Richard Moss

Richard Moss is the father of Aura and Peter Moss. He has three wives, including Zahra, whom he bought from her homeless mother when she was fifteen. Moss is an engineer for a big commercial water company. He has also put together his own form of religion, which emphasizes patriarchy and the subordination of women. Moss is killed when the neighborhood is overrun.

Zahra Moss

Zahra Moss is the youngest of Richard moss's three wives. Ross bought her from her homeless mother. Her new home is the first house she has lived in. When the neighborhood is destroyed, Zahra sees her baby daughter killed. But she escapes and heads north with Harry, who becomes her boyfriend. Zahra cannot read or write until Lauren starts to teach her.

Cory Olamina

Cory Olamina is Lauren's stepmother. An educated woman with a Ph.D., she teaches the neighborhood children. When the neighborhood deteriorates, she wants to move to Olivar but cannot persuade her husband to go. After her husband disappears, she takes over the teaching side of his job. Cory is killed when the neighborhood is attacked and burned.

Gregory Olamina

Gregory Olamina is Lauren's youngest brother. He is killed when the neighborhood is overrun.

Keith Olamina

Keith Olamina is the oldest of Lauren's three brothers and Cory's favorite, although he and Lauren do not get along well. He is twelve when the story begins. Keith is not very intelligent and dodges work and school whenever he can. His ambition is to leave the neighborhood and go to Los Angeles and make money. When he is thirteen, he frequently leaves the neighborhood for long periods. He acquires money and new clothes, but he will not say where he got them. After a few months of living dangerously, he is tortured and killed, possibly by the drug dealers he thought were his friends.

Lauren Olamina

Lauren Olamina is fifteen years old when the story begins. She lives in Robledo, California, with her father, stepmother, and three brothers. Her dead mother was taking the prescription drug Paracetco, and this was why Lauren contracted "hyperempathy syndrome," which means that she feels the physical pain of others in her own body. On the advice of her father, she tries to keep this condition secret, since she thinks she might be perceived as weak. She only confides in people she trusts.

Lauren is an academically gifted student. She finished her high school work early and has taken college-level courses. She also reads voraciously and is extremely well informed about history and current events. Although her father is a Baptist minister, Lauren has already lost her faith in the Christian God. She develops her own religion called Earthseed, based on the idea that God is Change. Change is her watchword. Even before disaster hits their community, she is certain that she does not want to live the life that is expected of her: to marry young, have children, and live in impoverished circumstances in Robledo. She also guesses that her neighborhood will be destroyed in the near future, and she makes plans to escape, reading everything she can about how to survive in emergency situations and how to live off the land.

When the disaster happens, Lauren shows that she is strong willed and determined and that she possesses great leadership qualities. She is the undisputed leader of the small group that heads north along the freeway, seeking a better life. She is ruthless, she kills when she has to, and she ensures that her group does what it has to do to survive. Gradually, she also instills in her companions a sense of ethics and community. Although she is tough, she also cares about others and shows compassion. She is rewarded when the group arrives at Bankole's land, where she can put her dream of founding an Earthseed community into practice.

Marcus Olamina

Marcus Olamina is Lauren's brother. At thirteen, he is already handsome, and he attracts girls. His friend is Robin Balter, Harry Balter's sister. Marcus is killed when the neighborhood is attacked.

Reverend Olamina

Reverend Olamina is Lauren's fifty-seven-year-old father and the husband of Cory. He is a college professor and dean and a Baptist minister. A very strict father, he severely beats Keith for misbehavior, which produces a permanent estrangement between father and son. He has also beaten Lauren, but she does not hold it against him. Reverend Olamina is a tough-minded man who does his best to protect his family in difficult circumstances. His own parents were murdered fifteen years earlier, and his first wife was a drug addict. Olamina goes missing from the neighborhood one day and is never found. He is presumed dead.

Wardell Parish

Wardell Parish is a strange and solitary man who lives in Lauren's neighborhood. His sister and all her children are killed in a house fire.

Justin Rohr

Justin Rohr is a three-year-old boy who is taken in by Lauren's group after his mother is killed just outside San Juan Bautista.

Emery Tanaka Solis

Emery Tanaka Solis is the twenty-three-year-old mother of Tori Solis. She married at thirteen and bore three children. After her husband died, she worked for an agribusiness conglomerate that made a virtual slave of her. She fell into debt, and the company took her two sons. She then fled with her daughter and headed north. They are taken in by Lauren's group toward the end of their trek.

Tori Solis

Tori is the nine-year-old daughter of Emery Tanaka Solis.

Curtis Talcott

Curtis Talcott is Lauren's boyfriend in Robledo. He wants to marry her and leave Robledo, but she says she must stay and help her family until she is eighteen. Although she says she will marry him if he waits for her, her heart is not in it. There is too much of herself that she is unable to share with him. She never sees him again after the neighborhood is attacked and burned, and she assumes he was killed, though she never knows for certain.

Kayla Talcott

Kayla Talcott is the mother of Curtis Talcott. After Reverend Olamina disappears, Kayla takes over some of his preaching and church work, even though she is not ordained.

Themes

Change

Lauren rejects traditional religion. Based on her experience, she sees no relevance in a belief system focused on the Christian God. Instead, she forms her own religion based on her observation that everything in the universe changes. Change is the one constant in life. People can either accept change and work with it for the betterment of themselves and their community, or they can resist it, hoping in vain that things will carry on the way they always have done.

For Lauren, change is God. This God shapes humans and is in turn shaped by them. God is dynamic process, not a static, transcendental lawgiver and judge. Change is an irresistible force, and humans can harness it to promote the spiritual evolution of the race. According Lauren's Earthseed religion, each human life is a seed that can sprout into something valuable and productive if it can adapt to changing realities. By yielding to change, this human earthseed can also shape it constructively. The consequences of failing to do so are death and chaos. The ultimate expression of Earthseed, its destiny, is "to take root among the stars," to spread human life to other planets and galaxies.

Topics for Further Study

- Research the history of illiteracy in the United States. What can be done to tackle illiteracy in the United States? How have educational methods developed over time to accommodate new finds or theories in literacy studies? Develop a political platform, a curriculum, or a tutorial that employs some of the methods for dealing with illiteracy that you encounter during your research. Try to propose some of your own resolutions and include them in your project.

- In the novel, water is scarce and expensive. Research the topic of water supply. Is water likely to become a scarce commodity in the twenty-first century? If so, what regions of the world already have this problem or will have this problem? Will the United States be affected and, if so, which areas?

- There are many sides in the current debate about global warming and climate change. Study the arguments about whether global warming is currently happening or not, about the effects of global warming on the environment as well as industry, and about who is responsible for helping industries comply with environmental sanctions aimed at reducing harmful emissions. Document your findings and prepare to debate with other members of your class by picking the argument with which you agree most and developing a strong defense for your position.

- Research the history of company towns in the United States in the nineteenth century. Write an essay that explains how your research compares with the description of Olivar in the novel. Is Butler's representation of Olivar historically accurate? Does the author leave out important elements that you found in your research? If so, what are those elements?

- Is Butler's pessimistic vision of America in the 2020s convincing? Are such developments likely or unlikely? Can you see ways in which America might develop differently?

Freedom

Lauren's trek north is a journey toward freedom. She is escaping the prison of a walled community in which there is no hope for a full, productive, free life. Most of the people her group accumulates on the way are fleeing from some kind of slavery or exploitation. Zahra Moss is escaping an oppressive marriage that rests on a belief in male superiority. Harry has turned down a chance to go to the company town of Olivar, in which the residents give up their freedom and their rights in order to buy security. Jill and Allie flee from a life of prostitution in which their pimp was their father; Travis and Natividad escape from menial service to a rich man who thought he had the right to seduce Natividad; Emery Solis and her daughter are escaping virtual slavery to an agribusiness that keeps them in permanent debt and even takes Emery's sons away. Bankole, too, is escaping from conditions of life similar to those that Lauren was enduring. He seeks freedom on the land he owns in the coastal hills. The members of Lauren's

Earthseed community who decide to settle there will at least be free to shape their own destiny, although there is no guarantee they will survive.

Loss and Restoration of Community

The novel is divided into two halves. The first half, set in Robledo, shows how the social order in California in 2024 has broken down. Society is split into several groups. The rich live in walled estates, with lavish security systems. The middle classes, much threatened and impoverished, live in walled communities and try to maintain a semblance of normal life. But jobs are scarce, and no one has any prospects. Inflation has eroded the value of money, and essentials such as water are expensive. In Lauren's neighborhood, people try to grow as much of their own food as they can. For meat, they rely on eating rabbits. Everyone in the community over the age of fifteen is trained in how to use guns, since they cannot rely on a corrupt police force for protection against the thieves who regularly break into their community. Outside, in unwalled areas, the rule of law and the sense of community have totally collapsed. Homeless, dirty, desperately poor people roam the streets, along with drunks and drug addicts. Many are addicted to a drug that makes them commit arson, because they love to watch things burn.

The second part of the novel presents a gradually emerging contrast between the lawlessness and brutality of life amongst the traveling bands of refugees and the sense of community and mutual responsibility that eventually characterizes Lauren's group. Lauren's quest is to recreate what an ideal community should be. At first, because of the dangerous situation she is in, she is ruthless, trusting no one and looking out only for herself and her two companions. But as she continues to travel north, she does not shut out the voice of compassion. A key moment is when she pulls Allie and Jill out of the rubble of a house. Bankole, who has never lost his sense of values, says to her, "I was surprised to see that anyone else cared what happened to a couple of strangers." Another key moment comes when Emery and her daughter are found in the group's camp. Lauren goes out of her way to feed them, offering them two of the five sweet pears that she had bought only two days earlier. Seeing her example, other members of the group share what food they have. When Lauren puts out the idea that Emery and the girl could join their group, Harry tells her she is going soft. "You would have raised hell if we'd tried to take in a beggar woman and her child a few weeks ago." But Lauren is not going soft. She is simply demonstrating that in spite of the degradation and danger all around her, humans can still show that they care about each other. Then, when Jill is killed, Lauren comforts the grief-stricken Allie with a hug. The message she conveys is "*In spite of your loss and pain, you aren't alone. You still have people who care about you and want you to be all right. You still have family.*" When Lauren's new "family," a heterogeneous, multiracial group that spans several generations, arrives at their destination, they have learned to take care of each other. They are ready to develop a community based not on fear or exploitation but on mutual respect and shared values.

Style

Dystopia

A dystopia is an unpleasant, sometimes frightening, imaginary future world. Dystopias usually take undesirable aspects of present-day society and depict a world in which those aspects have become dominant. In *Parable of the Sower*, Butler creates a dystopia by magnifying some disturbing social trends that occurred in the United States in the late 1980s and early 1990s. These trends included the widespread use of designer drugs (custom-made, mind-altering drugs such as Ecstasy). In the novel, use of the drug pyro reaches epidemic proportions. It makes people commit arson because doing so feels better than sex. Another trend in the 1990s was the increasing popularity, particularly in California, of gated communities protected by security fences. These become the walled communities in 2024 California. In both cases, the walls go up because of fear of crime. Homelessness, illiteracy, and global warming were other issues in the 1990s that appear in larger form in the novel.

Image and Metaphor

The novel takes its title from the parable of the sower in the gospel of Luke. The sower is like the spiritual teacher who spreads the word of truth.

Some people listen; others do not—just as seeds take root in some places but not in others. In the *New Testament*, the sower is Jesus; in the novel, it is Lauren. The metaphor of the seed occurs again in the name Lauren gives to her new religion, Earthseed. It is also reflected in the name of the first Earthseed community: Acorn. The acorn image occurs earlier in the novel, too. Lauren loves to eat bread made with acorns rather than wheat or rye. Her father tells her that he had a difficult time persuading his neighbors to eat acorns. They wanted to cut down the oak trees and plant something else they considered more useful. Lauren learns from a book how to make acorn bread, and this helps to sustain their group as they travel north. The acorn image conveys the idea that the seeds of new life are always available, not only in nature but in humans, too.

Historical Context

Illiteracy

Rising rates of illiteracy became a matter of public concern in America in the late 1980s and early 1990s. In 1989, it was estimated that 13 percent of seventeen-year-old Americans could not read or write and that twenty million Americans had problems with literacy. Some could not read or write at all, and this often resulted from poverty or being in culturally disadvantaged families. Others were partially literate and could read street signs and grocery lists but not much more. Often this was due to undiagnosed learning disorders such as dyslexia. According to a 1987 National Assessment of Educational Progress government survey, although 96 percent of those between twenty-one and twenty-five years old had basic reading skills, less than 48 percent were capable of reading a map well enough to use it properly. In the 1993 National Adult Literacy Survey by the Department of Education, over 40 percent of the adult population fell short of the literacy skills needed to succeed on a day-to-day basis.

Gated Communities

In the late 1980s, fear of rising crime in urban areas led to a growth in the number of gated residential communities in the United States, particularly in California and other western and southern metropolitan areas. These were communities where access was controlled through gates and security guards. Sometimes fences topped with barbed wire surrounded the community. An example of a gated community is Canyon Lake, located seventy miles east of Los Angeles. Created in 1968, it incorporated as a city of its own in 1990. Gated communities proved an effective deterrent against crime, and their numbers increased throughout the United States in the 1990s. In 1997, there were about twenty thousand gated communities, which increased to around fifty thousand by 2000.

Fear of Crime

Fear of crime was a prominent feature of life in the United States at the time *Parable of the Sower* was written. According to a 1994 Gallup Poll, 52 percent of the people in the United States named crime as the most important social problem, up from only 9 percent in a similar poll conducted eighteen months earlier. A 1993 poll showed that 87 percent of U.S. residents thought that crime was higher than a year earlier. This was not in fact true, since the crime rate fell from 1991 to 1994, but people thought it was true. There was a particularly strong fear in urban areas of street crime and random, gang-related violence. Fear of crime led legislators and the public at large to call for harsher punishments for criminals. In California, a "three strikes" law was passed in 1994. It mandated a sentence of twenty-five years to life for a third felony conviction if the previous felonies were serious or violent.

Homelessness

Homelessness in America increased drastically during the 1980s, to an estimated two million people in 1989. Some experts argue that the policies of the Reagan administration were to blame for cutting welfare programs and making massive cuts in the budget of the Department of Housing and Urban Development (HUD). HUD was the main government sponsor of subsidized housing for the poor. The situation was not helped by the fact that poverty also increased during the 1980s. In 1978, 24.5 million people lived below the federal poverty line; by 1988 this had risen to 32.5 million. The gap between rich and poor also increased. Another factor in the rise of homelessness in the 1980s arose from concerns about the rights of the mentally ill. It became harder to commit people to mental hospitals against their will. The result was that many mentally ill people ended up on the streets. It is estimated that one-third of the homeless during the 1980s were mentally ill and that a similar proportion had problems with substance abuse.

Climate Change

Concerns about global warming, an increase in Earth's average surface temperature, were first raised in the 1980s. The phenomenon was also known as the "greenhouse effect." Many scientists believed that global warning was caused by an increase in emissions of gases such as carbon dioxide resulting from the burning of fossil fuels for energy production. In 1988, James Hansen, director of the Goddard Institute for Space Studies at NASA, told a U.S. Senate committee there was strong evidence that global warming was being caused by human activity. He warned that if global warming were not reversed, it would cause catastrophic climatic changes. Throughout the 1990s, scientists warned of extreme weather including floods, heat waves, droughts, and hurricanes that would occur as a result of global warning.

Critical Overview

Although Four Walls Eight Windows, the original publishers of *Parable of the Sower*, tried to present the book as similar to the fiction of other African American writers such as Toni Morrison and Toni Cade Bambara, reviewers seemed still to regard it as science fiction. This did not prevent the novel from receiving high praise. For Faren Miller, in *Locus*, it "presents what is simply the most emotionally and intellectually appealing religion I've encountered in nearly four decades of reading sf." Miller commented on the grim nature of the world depicted and the religious issues Butler presents but added that the novel "functions beautifully as fiction, brimming with living characters and the crazy complexity of life."

Hoda Zaki, in *Women's Review of Books*, pointed out that Butler drew extensively on African American history:

> [I]mages of slavery remind us of the U.S. past: slaves hiding their attempts at self-education and literacy, and fleeing cruel overseers; Lauren's band of survivors, which recalls the Underground Railroad; the pervasive feeling that freedom, work and security lie to the north.

Zaki also pointed out that Butler shows characters from a variety of racial backgrounds in positive roles that are not usually found in science fiction novels about the future. Zaki concluded, "In a world increasingly polarized ethnically and racially, [Butler's] work contributes a needed critical element to the genre of science fiction."

In a glowing review in the *New York Times Book Review*, Gerald Jonas commented that although religious awakenings are common in science fiction of the future, they are often arbitrary and conventional, but Butler "dares to take Lauren's revelations seriously," and this enables her to show how Lauren's ideas capture the allegiance of her followers. Jonas concluded that the novel succeeded on many levels: "A gripping tale of survival and a poignant account of growing up sane in a disintegrating world, it is at bottom a subtle and disturbing exposition of the gospel according to Lauren."

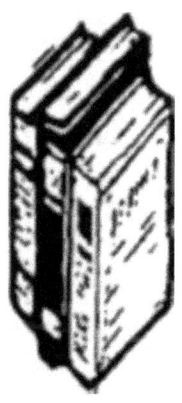

What Do I Read Next?

- *Parable of the Talents* (1998) is Butler's sequel to *Parable of the Sower*. The Earthseed community that Lauren founded is collapsing. Her followers are enslaved, her daughter is kidnapped, and she is imprisoned by religious fanatics. But Lauren continues to believe in Earthseed and must find a way for the Acorn community to survive.

- Neal Stephenson's bestselling *Snow Crash* (1992) is a fast-paced, near-future dystopia, in which the United States is a collection of city-states controlled by corporations and the Mafia controls pizza delivery. The hero, named Hiro Protagonist, is a computer hacker (and samurai swordsman) who battles with a deadly designer drug called Snow Crash, that is also a sinister, world-endangering computer virus.

- *A Clockwork Orange* (1962), by Anthony Burgess, is a grim dystopia narrated by Alex, a member of an extremely violent teenage gang. When Alex is imprisoned, he is subjected to a new government-sponsored treatment program designed to cure his violent behavior. He comes out of it as a model citizen but has no free will nor the capacity to do good or experience pleasure.

- *The Handmaid's Tale: A Novel* (1986), by Margaret Atwood, is a near-future fable in which the United States has become the Republic of Gilead, controlled by religious fundamentalists. Women are strictly controlled and have no rights. Atwood's target is the Christian right's views about the proper role of women. She attempts to show what might happen if such views are taken to their logical conclusion.

Sources

Johnson, Rebecca O., "African-American, Feminist Science Fiction," in *Sojourner: The Women's Forum*, Vol. 19, No. 6, February 1994, pp. 12–14.

Jonas, Gerald, Review of *Parable of the Sower*, in *New York Times Book Review*, January 2, 1994, p. 22.

Miller, Faren, Review of *Parable of the Sower*, in *Locus*, December 1993, pp. 17, 19.

See, Lisa, "An Interview with Octavia Butler," in *Publishers Weekly*, Vol. 240, No. 50, December 13, 1993, pp. 50–51.

Zaki, Hoda, Review of *Parable of the Sower*, in *Women's Review of Books*, Vol. 11, Nos. 10 and 11, July 1994, pp. 37–38.

Further Reading

Butler, Octavia, and Stephen W. Potts, "'We Keep Playing the Same Record': A Conversation with Octavia E. Butler," in *Science-Fiction Studies*, Vol. 23, No. 70, November 1996, pp. 331–38.

> Butler discusses the science-fiction genre, responses to her work, and themes her work addresses.

Fry, Joan, "An Interview with Octavia Butler," in *Poets & Writers Magazine*, Vol. 25, March/April 1997, pp. 58–69.

> Butler discusses a range of topics, including her favorite writers and where the philosophical ideas in *Parable of the Sower* come from.

Wiloch, Thomas, Review of *Parable of the Sower*, in *Bloomsbury Review*, May/June 1994, p. 24.

> Wiloch applauds Butler for not following the pattern of most science fiction. She is not content to tell a standard adventure story but instead turns it into a character study of a young woman.

CPSIA information can be obtained
at www.ICGtesting.com
Printed in the USA
LVHW080056210721
693260LV00022B/846